Thank You
For
Everything
SCHOOL

Made in the USA
Middletown, DE
26 October 2022

13556339R00064